What's a Frank Frank?

Tasty Homograph Riddles

by Giulio Maestro

My Name Is Frank! What's Yours?

CLARION BOOKS
NEW YORK

Clarion Books
a Houghton Mifflin Company imprint
215 Park Avenue South, New York, NY 10003
Copyright © 1984 by Giulio Maestro
All rights reserved.
For information about permission to reproduce
selections from this book, write to Permissions,
Houghton Mifflin Company, 2 Park Street, Boston, MA 02108
Printed in the USA

Library of Congress Cataloging in Publication Data
Maestro, Giulio.
What's a frank frank?
Summary: A collection of original riddles making
use of homographs, words that are spelled the same
but have different meanings.
1. Riddles, Juvenile.   2. Puns and punning.
[1. Riddles.   2. Puns and punning.   3. English
language — Homonyms]   I. Title.
PN6371.5.M3   1984   818'.5402   84-5021
RNF ISBN 0-89919-297-1
PAP ISBN 0-89919-317-X

WOZ 10 9 8 7 6 5 4

The question is:
What's a homograph?

Suppose you are reading a book, and you find the same word in two places in the story. The first time it means one thing, and the next time it means something else. But it is spelled the same way in both places.

What have you found? You've found a homograph, two words that are written the same way but have different meanings. Sometimes homographs are pronounced differently. But when they are pronounced the same way, they are also a type of homophone or homonym.

Frank frank is an example of a homophonic homograph, and there are sixty more of them in the riddles in this book. In fact, the book is just riddled with homographs.

What's a frank frank?

A hot dog who gives his honest opinion.

Who can hide in her hide?

A turtle.

What's a rank rank?

A smelly row of garbage cans.

How do you hail hail?

Greet falling lumps of ice.

What's a class with class?

Students with style.

Why did the duck duck the angry bee?

He didn't want to get the point.

How do you foil a foil foil?

Fend off an attack by an aluminum sword.

What is a fleet fleet?

A bunch of fast ships.

Who is the sire of the sire of the future sire?

The grandfather of the prince.

When does a trunk carry a trunk?

When an elephant goes on vacation.

How do you field a flying field?

Catch an airport when it's thrown to you!

What's a pupil pupil?

An eye school student.

Who nails some nails but not other nails?

Someone who doesn't hammer her fingers.

When does a batter beat batter?

When a baseball player makes pancakes.

When do bows make bows?

When polite ships meet.

What are rails on rails who rail at each other?

Angry birds riding trains.

How can you spell spells for a spell?

Write magic words for a while.

What's a spare spare?

A skinny extra tire.

When is the Pacific pacific?

When the ocean is calm.

How do you park at a park?

Stop your car at a public garden.

What peeps and peeps through a crack?

A chick.

What get worn out as they're worn?

Shoes.

Why couldn't the tackle tackle tackle?

The football player couldn't deal with fishing gear.

What's a whitecap that's a swell swell?

A terrific ocean wave.

How do you spruce up a spruce?

Dress up an evergreen tree.

When does a steer steer?

When an ox drives a car.

Who are trolls who troll while they troll?

Fairy-tale characters who sing as they fish.

When does a tap tap-dance?

When a faucet performs to music.

What's a sash with a sash?

A window with a pretty cloth wound around it.

What's a scoop about a scoop?

A big story about ice cream.

What is a perch on a perch?

A fish who thinks she's a bird on a branch.

How does a shed shed snow?

The slanted roof makes it slide off.

What is a yard yard?

A nine-foot-square garden.

How is a sole sole like a sole?

One flat fish is like the bottom of a shoe.

What is a shaft in a shaft?

A ray of light in a miner's tunnel.

What are the squalls of squalls?

Screaming winds of sudden storms.

What's a cord inside a cord?

A stack of firewood tied with rope.

Who can shift in a shift?

A driver in a summer dress.

What's a row of pigs who row?

A line of boars using oars.

When are scales on scales?

When fish are getting weighed.

When was the chimney swift swift?

When the bird flew out of the flue in a hurry.

What's a meal meal?

A dinner of grain.

Who stole away after he stole the stole?

The robber who made off with the fur cape.

When is stock stock-still?

When cattle stand motionless.

Who says, "The mine is mine!"?

A prospector staking a claim.

Why did the tender feel tender?

The engine had bumped it.

How can you jar a jar?

Shake up some jam.

How did a bill give a bill to pay a bill?

A bird used his beak to pay for his fruit.

When does Santa fume about fumes?

When he can't get past the smoke.

When is a groom a groom?

When a horse's caretaker gets married.

How does a hungry caterpillar stalk a stalk?

He goes after the stem of a plant.

How do you pass through a pass?

Drive between two mountains.

Who hacks wood except when he hacks?

A lumberjack with a bad cough.

What's a hound who likes to hound you?

A pest of a dog.

What's a hammock in a hammock?

A swinging net in a stand of trees.

How do you skirt a skirt?

Just walk around a dress.

What's a charm that works like a charm?

A piece of jewelry that's enchanting.

What's a clutch in a clutch?

A bunch of eggs in a tight spot.

What's the opposite of a low low?

A high moo.

What's a clip at a fast clip?

A haircut that's short and swift.

When do pages turn pages?

When the king's helpers read him a book.